WEST COUNTRY BRANCH LINES
A Colour Portfolio

Peter W. Gray

Ian Allan PUBLISHING

Introduction

Welcome to a further selection of pictures from my branch line colour portfolio. This time I am commencing a little farther east, in Gloucestershire, before taking a look at selected branch lines in the south-west peninsular, travelling in a generally westward direction, down through Somerset, Devon and Cornwall.

You will find that some of the pictures have been arranged in pairs, illustrating either contrasting, opposing or even similar views, taken at or near the same location.

The panoramic views seem to have been popular with the readers of previous volumes, at least with those with whom I have had contact, so there are a few additions this time, as well as the return of an old friend, albeit using a different slide from that used before.

I have often noticed, when looking at other people's old photographs, that with the passing of the years, it is often something in the background of the picture, that is now of more interest than the main subject, for which it was originally taken. Possibly this is why my long distance views are, or seem to be, popular, because they contain so much more information, different aspects of which will interest different people.

I started taking colour slides in 1957, by which time I was already a member of the Railway Correspondence & Travel Society's Pictorial and Technical Travelling Portfolio, and it was perhaps fortuitous that I also joined the local camera club. The former gave me an insight into the standards being achieved by other railway photographers in black and white prints, while the latter soon taught me the basic elements of composition, which apply to all forms of art, not just to photography.

Using the fixed-lens cameras of those days, although restricting in many ways, did, I feel sure, enable us to cope with the very slow film speed of Kodachrome I, on which many of these pictures were recorded. When using a modern single lens reflex camera, you lose the view while the shutter is open. However, in those days the fixed-lens cameras had separate viewfinders, so that you could still concentrate on a fixed point in the view all the way through a relatively long exposure. Otherwise how could I have got away with one of the pictures in this selection, exposed at one fifteenth of a second — held in the hand. I will leave you to guess which one it was, but it needed plenty of 'depth of field'.

Front cover: The Newton Abbot bankers were not always as clean as this, but on 30 March 1962 2-6-2T No 5153 is on a 'semi-Royal' duty, conveying Princess Margaret on a private visit to Torquay. Two ex-GWR Special Saloons are attached to the rear of the Kingswear portion of the 2.30pm from Paddington, which has also been strengthened at the front, and is passing Aller Pottery.

Back cover: 0-4-2T No 1466 is northbound out of Tiverton on the Exe Valley line with the 3.22pm from Exeter St David's to Dulverton on 24 March 1962.

Title page: On a day of heavy showers the crew of 2-6-0 No 6327 have the weather-sheet deployed to improve the limited protection provided by the Churchward cab. The 4.10pm from Barnstaple Junction to Taunton is pulling away from Morebath Junction Halt on 13 April 1963.

First published 2003

ISBN 0 7110 2950 4

© Peter W. Gray 2003

Published by Ian Allan Publishing

an imprint of Ian Allan Publishing Ltd, Hersham, Surrey KT12 4RG.
Printed by Ian Allan Printing Ltd, Hersham, Surrey KT12 4RG.

Code: 0306/B2

For the record, the cameras I used were a Voigtlander Vito IIa with a f3.5 Color-Skopar lens until early in 1959, when I moved on to a Agfa Super Silette with f2 Solagon lens. This was replaced by a Pentax S1a, with interchangeable lens, in the Spring of 1965.

While compiling the captions I had occasion to seek additional information from Derek Frost and Eric Youldon, to whom thanks are due, also to Peter Waller and his colleagues at Ian Allan Publishing, and not forgetting Derek Huntriss, who converts my somewhat erratic typing into the elegant script you see before you.

Lastly, thanks to all the West Country railwaymen and women, who went about their tasks so effectively, often in far from salubrious conditions, and made it all possible.

Peter W. Gray
Torquay
February 2003

On the track of what is now the Paignton & Dartmouth Steam Railway, 4-6-0 No 4098 *Kidwelly Castle* climbs towards Churston on 27 June 1961 with the four coach Kingswear portion of the 1.30pm from Paddington to Penzance, the 'Royal Duchy'. This has been strengthened at the front with two non-corridor coaches, probably for tomorrow's school train from Kingswear. In the foreground Waterside Caravan Park lies in the hollow, while across the waters of Torbay can be seen some of the seven hills of Torquay, still then clad in Victorian villas.

Left: It is cold but clear on 24 November 1962, as 0-4-2T No 1453 approaches Tramway Crossing, alongside the ex-GWR Gloucester locomotive depot, with a well-filled auto coach bound for Chalford. In the background a 'Castle' class 4-6-0 is backing off shed and two '5101' class 2-6-2Ts are queueing at the coal stage.

Although not strictly a branch line, the Chalford autos provided a frequent branch line style service from Gloucester to the stations and halts between Stonehouse and Chalford.

Above: With only another week to go before the Chalford auto service was to be withdrawn, 0-4-2T No 1453 is pulling away from Brimscombe with the 3.8pm from Gloucester on 24 October 1964. Behind the train can be seen the stark remains of the then recently demolished engine shed, which had housed banking engines since the earliest days of the GWR, to assist loaded coal trains on the stiff climb to Sapperton tunnel.

Above: Beyond the roof of Bristol (Temple Meads) train shed, enthusiasts attempt to improve the rather grubby appearance of 2-6-2T No 5532, before it works the final 2.53pm Saturdays only service to Frome, over the North Somerset line on 31 October 1959. On the centre road 4-6-0 No 6028 *King George VI*, with the 'Merchant Venturer' headboard reversed, prepares to take over the 2.15pm from Weston-super-Mare to Paddington, which has arrived on the adjacent track.

Right: On a Sunday afternoon, some of the engines which worked over the North Somerset line, serving the local quarries and coal mines, could be found at Frome, a sub-shed of Westbury. On 7 June 1959 2-6-2Ts Nos 4555, 5508 and 5542 were present, together with 0-6-0PTs Nos 3614, 4636, 5757, 7784 and 9668. Note the ex-GWR Automatic Train Control test ramps on both exit roads from the shed area.

Above: It is 1.25pm on Saturday 31 October 1959 as 4-6-0 No 4971 *Stanway Hall* runs into Yatton with the Saturdays only 12.25pm from Taunton to Bristol (Temple Meads). In the far distance can be seen the tail of the Saturdays only 12.55pm from Bristol (Temple Meads) to Weston-super-Mare, hauled by 4-6-0 No 5954 *Faendre Hall*. Both trains are connecting with the 1.30pm Clevedon branch train, consisting of 0-4-2T No 1463 and auto trailers Nos 233 and 227. In the middle distance is Yatton West signalbox, of Bristol & Exeter Railway origin, while curving away to the left is the Cheddar Valley line.

Right: The Cheddar Valley line connected Yatton in the west, with Witham to the east, via Cheddar and Wells.

Sandford & Banwell was the second station out, and Ivatt 2-6-2T No 41202 is making a vigorous departure with the Saturdays only 1.15pm from Yatton to Wells on 4 March 1961. The mileage on this line was measured from the Witham end.

Above: At 10.40am on 21 July 1962, Ivatt 2-6-2T No 41242 draws into Pylle Halt with only the second train of the day from Highbridge for Burnham-on-Sea, this one bound for Templecombe. The once-tidy roses around the lamp column are rampant, but the loop line has gone and the signalbox is deserted.

Right: Looking north at Evercreech Junction, an afternoon train disappears towards Highbridge, on what was once the main line of the Somerset Central Railway. When this met the Dorset Central at Cole in February 1862, a coast-to-coast line was complete, which later that year became the Somerset & Dorset Railway. On completion of the Bath extension in July 1874 (curving around to the right) this then became the Somerset & Dorset main line, with the Highbridge and Burnham line now relegated to branch status.

On 3 January 1966, the foreground entrance tracks to the sorting sidings are already abandoned, as Ivatt 2-6-2T No 41290 threads its way through a wondrous variety of signals.

Two views from the road bridge overlooking Yeovil (Pen Mill) station, both taken on 30 May 1964.

At 12.35pm a diesel multiple unit forming the 11.40am Weymouth to Westbury service has arrived to connect with the Saturdays only 12.37pm to Taunton, hauled by 2-6-2T No 4591.

Later that afternoon, BR Standard Class 5 4-6-0 No 73042 had arrived at 3.10pm with the 2.0pm stopping service from Weymouth, which terminated here. It has now backed out of the station onto the down Weymouth line, to clear the way for the return of No 4591 on the 2.10pm (SO) from Taunton, which was one minute late at 3.25pm.

It is now raining as No 4591 shunts its coaches across to the down side, clearing the up track for the 3.0pm from Weymouth to Bristol. The Class 5 will take an 'all stations' service to Westbury at 3.55pm, and No 4591 will return to Taunton at 4.0pm.

Above: Towards the end of a busy Saturday 24 August 1963 B-B Hymek diesel-hydraulic No D7007 pilots 2-6-2T No 6113 on the climb to Crowcombe, with the 4.20pm from Minehead to Taunton. Both engines had already made at least two return trips between Taunton and Minehead that Saturday. No 6113 had worked in on the 9.45am Minehead to Manchester, and returned with the 8.50am from Swansea, while D7007 worked out on the 9.43am from Taunton, returned with the 11.15am Minehead to Paddington, and then picked up the 10.15am from Paddington (1.25pm from Taunton) to Minehead.

Right: At Taunton station on Saturday 11 August 1962, 2-6-0 No 7326 on the 11.45 am to Barnstaple Junction, looks out from the bay as 2-6-2T No 4143 leaves with the through coaches to Minehead, off the 8.15am from Paddington. Try counting the semaphore signal arms visible in this shot.

Left: Wearing the express headlamp code, and hardly troubled by its three packed Southern Region coaches, 2-6-0 No 6345 pulls away from Wiveliscombe with the 7.55am from Ilfracombe to Taunton on Saturday 25 July 1964. During the construction of the Devon & Somerset Railway from Norton Fitzwarren to Barnstaple, Wiveliscombe was reached in June 1871 and remained the terminus until November 1873, when the whole line was opened through to Barnstaple.

Above: Who will get to Barnstaple first? On the climb from Milverton to Wiveliscombe the single track of the Barnstaple branch ran for a short stretch right alongside the then main A361 road to north Devon. The cars are nose-to-tail as 2-6-0 No 6363 steams past with the 11.25am from Taunton to Barnstaple Junction on Saturday 25 July 1964.

Other engines working on this line that day, all Moguls, were Nos 7303, 7306, 7337 and Southern Region 'N' class No 31406.

A panoramic view looking down the Slade valley into Ilfracombe as the double-headed summer Saturday 12 noon to London Waterloo pulls out alongside the white-roofed engine shed on 27 July 1963. The pilot engine is a 'N' class Mogul, probably No 31856, but the 'West Country / Battle of Britain' class Pacific train engine was not identified. The 7.50am from Yeovil Town, due in at 12.5pm, is approaching and the road has already been cleared for its arrival. Twenty minutes later, ex-SR 'N' class 2-6-0 No 31838 piloted ex-GWR 2-6-0 No 6346 out of Ilfracombe with the 12.25pm to Taunton.

The opposing view to that on the opposite page, looking up the fierce 1 in 37 climb out of Ilfracombe on Saturday 30 June 1962. On the left, heading the 2.55pm to Waterloo, three coaches and a bogie van, are Bulleid Pacifics No 34066 *Spitfire* and No 34011 *Tavistock*. At the station throat, 'N' class 2-6-0 No 31839 has just arrived 'light engine' from Mortehoe, while in the carriage sidings sister engine No 31849 is station pilot.

Left: Churchward 2-6-0 No 7304 almost appears to be about to omit its booked stop at Morebath Junction Halt, as the 4.20pm from Taunton to Barnstaple Junction races in on 13 April 1963. Some of the potential passengers are taking shelter from a heavy shower.

Above: Looking down on Morebath Junction, the line to Taunton runs through a shallow cutting out of the right side of this picture towards Morebath station. The Exe Valley line — already closed when this view was taken on 31 January 1964 — comes in from the left on a sweeping curve to join the line to Barnstaple, which, after passing through Morebath Junction Halt, disappears off to the left.

A view for the modellers of the back of Tiverton Junction signalbox, as 0-4-2T No 1471 shunts meat containers into the Cattle Pens siding on 1 June 1963. A further line of containers partially obscures the engine shed, which normally housed overnight the 0-4-2Ts working the Culm Valley and Tiverton branches.

In the warm rays of a rapidly sinking sun, 0-4-2T No 1421 arrives
back at Tiverton Junction on 3 November 1962, with the 2.45pm from
Hemyock; four loaded milk tanks and the passenger coach.

23

Left: Both this and the facing picture were taken on the afternoon of 8 June 1963, which although a beautiful summer's day, was for the railway still the penultimate Saturday of the winter service. This is Thorverton, which was typical of the stations along the Exe Valley line, serving the villages which were mostly situated on higher ground, away from the Exe flood plain. On leaving the station the line towards Tiverton curves around and crosses the river, making for Up Exe Halt, which is hidden in the trees.

Below us, 0-4-2T No 1466 propelling the 5.15pm from Dulverton has been awaiting the arrival of 0-6-0PT No 3659 with the 5.48pm from Exeter St David's.

Above: From almost the same viewpoint, we see 0-4-2T No 1451 approaching with the 4.25pm from Exeter St David's to Tiverton, which on weekdays went through to Bampton.

In this direction we are looking towards the confluence of the Exe and Culm valleys, just beyond the already closed Stoke Canon station, and the main line trains, by then mostly diesel-hydraulic hauled, could be seen and heard in the distance.

Only four months earlier, this landscape had been snow-covered, and the river Exe frozen from bank to bank at this point.

Due to a temporary shortage of diesel railcars during February 1965, steam was reinstated on the Lyme Regis branch for a short time. Down in 'Happy Valley', the cackle of the chickens scratching around their coops is temporarily drowned by the exhaust from Ivatt 2-6-2T No 41216, as it accelerates its single Western Region auto trailer across Cannington viaduct and on up to Combpyne on 27 February 1965.

Sidmouth Junction on summer Saturdays could be the scene of intense activity, both these engines having arrived separately with through coaches for Waterloo from Exmouth and Sidmouth within the last hour, are now setting out together with the 11.45am from Waterloo to Sidmouth and Exmouth on 10 August 1963, which will split at Tipton St John's.

On the main line the Exmouth coaches had been taken forward to Waterloo by BR Standard Class 5 4-6-0 No 73088 *Joyous Gard*, and the Sidmouth coaches by Bulleid Pacific No 35001 *Channel Packet*, working the 11.48am Plymouth to Waterloo from Exeter Central.

In the down direction, Bulleid 'West Country' 4-6-2 No 34009 *Lyme Regis* had brought in the 11.45am from Waterloo, which, after reversal, is being taken down the branch by Ivatt 2-6-2T No 41307 and BR Standard Class 4 2-6-4T No 80042.

Above: The approach to Exmouth on the now closed line from Tipton St John's and Budleigh Salterton on 2 November 1963, behind BR Standard Class 4 2-6-4T No 80041, presents an unusual view of Starcross, across the Exe estuary, backed by the Haldon hills.

Right: It was across the Haldon hills that the Teign Valley line climbed from City Basin Junction (Exeter) to terminate at Heathfield on the Moretonhampstead branch.

This is Heathfield at 10.42am on 7 June 1958, the 'last day' for passenger services on the Teign Valley line, and the very last time three passenger trains would be here together. 0-4-2T No 1466 is leaving with the 10.5am from Paignton to Moretonhampstead, 2-6-2T No 5164 is almost ready to leave for Newton Abbot with the 10.15am from Moretonhampstead and in the bay platform, 2-6-2T No 5536 waits on the 10.43am Teign Valley service to Exeter.

Left: Also on 7 June 1958 0-4-2T No 1466 is seen returning from Moretonhampstead with the 11.35am departure, coasting down from Lustleigh into Pullabrook Halt. The signs on the right indicate the presence of a footpath down the embankment and across the rails to the platform on the down side.

Above: With less than two months to go before closure to passengers, 0-4-2T No 1466 is again on duty. This time with only a single auto trailer, it is crossing the heathland beyond Heathfield with the 12.50pm from Newton Abbot to Moretonhampstead on 3 January 1959. During the Civil War a battle was fought hereabouts, but sadly today an industrial estate covers most of the heathland.

On peak summer Saturdays the Kingswear branch carried more trains than the main line to Plymouth, though not many of them stopped at the first station, Kingskerswell, here being passed by 4-6-0 No 5032 *Usk Castle* with train No 1C74, the 10.20am from Paddington to Paignton on 5 August 1961.

Newton Abbot had several of these Hawksworth pannier tanks allocated, and like some other sheds, had difficulty finding enough work for them, as they were too heavy for most of the branch lines. However, the Kingswear branch was up to main line standards and on

18 April 1960 0-6-0PT No 9487 is making a spirited climb out of Torre station with the 8.0am Kingswear to Manchester coaches, which will join the 8.0am Plymouth to Liverpool coaches at Newton Abbot.

At 5.22pm on 30 April 1960, dead on time, the three Manchester to Kingswear coaches off the 9.5am Liverpool to Plymouth service are approaching the Torquay Gas Works signalbox, between Torquay and Paignton, behind 'Castle' class 4-6-0 No 5066 *Sir Felix Pole*. Until 1910 there had been a single line tunnel here, which extended to the bridge in the background.

Following the closure of the Moretonhampstead branch passenger service, the South Devon Railway Society was formed with preservation in mind. On 6 June 1960 the society ran the 'Heart of Devon Rambler' from Paignton to Moretonhampstead and back. This was hauled by 2-6-2T No 4174 and the engine is being prepared for the journey while standing in Paignton station.

Left: 4-6-0 No 6874 *Houghton Grange*, from Taunton, is stepping out across Broadsands viaduct with the 9.10am 'all stations' service from Exeter to Kingswear on 11 March 1960. This train was booked for a seven minute stop at Dawlish Warren, while being overtaken by the 7.40am from Bristol to Plymouth, and would not have called at Goodrington Sands Halt, which was not due to open for the summer season until 2 May.

Above: Later that day, at Churston station, the driver of the Brixham auto poses alongside 0-4-2T No 1470 as 'Castle' class 4-6-0 No 5055 *Earl of Eldon* pulls away with the Kingswear portion of the up 'Cornishman' express. At Exeter the Kingswear and Penzance portions will be combined, and *Earl of Eldon* will take the whole train through to Bristol.

With the closure of the Ashburton branch to all traffic imminent, this was the occasion of the running of the last annual Buckfastleigh Combined Sunday Schools Excursion train to Teignmouth, which took place on 1 August 1962. In this view the eight coach formation of empty stock is approaching Nursery Pool bridge on the way to Buckfastleigh behind 2-6-2Ts Nos 4574 and 4567.

In this view, the same 2-6-2Ts, now in the reverse order, are bringing the excursion train, now loaded with excited and expectant youngsters, into the down platform road at Totnes.

Here the train will reverse and 4-6-0 No 5003 *Lulworth Castle* will take it over Dainton summit and on to Teignmouth. The empty stock will be taken to Exminster sidings and the 'Castle' will go on to Exeter for servicing.

In the evening the whole procedure will be reversed, to get the passengers back to Buckfastleigh.

Two pictures from the early days of preservation.

Left: On 14 May 1966 Dart Valley Railway 0-4-2T No 1420 is gently propelling its train from Buckfastleigh back to Ashburton, over the section of the line now buried beneath the new A38 trunk road.

Above: Three months later, in the Cattle Market sidings, off the Totnes Quay line, on 21 August 1966 the Great Western Society is having an Open Day. Both 4-6-0 No 6998 *Burton Agnes Hall* and the little 0-6-0ST dock shunter No 1363 are in steam, and behind is the last example of a Churchward 'Dreadnought' bogie coach. All this stock is now at the Society's Didcot Railway Centre.

Two contrasting views of Gara Bridge station, the only crossing point on the Kingsbridge branch.

Above: 2-6-2T No 4561 is taking the 2.30pm from Brent out of Gara Bridge towards Kingsbridge on 29 April 1961, and about to make one of several crossings of the river Avon.

Alongside the down platform are the two Camping Coaches then stationed at Gara Bridge. In 1960 these were Nos 9895 and 9925, with paint dates of 2/59 and 12/59 respectively, but by 1961 No 9895 had been replaced by No 9909, a veteran vehicle originally built back in 1903.

Right: On a perfect Spring day, 26 March 1960, 2-6-2T No 5558 has stopped to exchange single line tokens, while running 'light engine' from Kingsbridge to Brent. The beautifully maintained gardens were a feature of many stations in those days.

Both of these views of Kingsbridge station were taken from the field above the station on 3 June 1961, only a week before the end of 100% steam operation.

Left: 2-6-2T No 4561, a regular on the branch in 1960 and 1961, appears to be departing at high speed, but is in fact only carrying out a shunting movement, and will soon return to dispose of the coach in the carriage shed.

Above: In those days I suffered badly with hay fever, and getting this close to the long grass in June was asking for trouble! The fireman on 2-6-2T No 5573 is just starting to rouse the fire, before setting out from Kingsbridge with the 12.20pm 'mixed' train to Brent. The 'mixed' portion of the train consisted only of a brake van.

Left: For six years, between the completion of the South Devon & Tavistock Railway in June 1859, and its continuation as the Launceston & South Devon Railway in July 1865, Tavistock station was a terminus. In its final years Tavistock South remained a terminus for the auto train services from Plymouth, and on 23 June 1962, 0-6-0PT No 6430 is ready to depart back to Plymouth, with an empty stock working at 2.0pm.

Above: Lydford station, on the edge of Dartmoor, was the summit of the Launceston extension, being 650ft above sea level. 2-6-2T No 4555 has arrived with the Saturdays only 10.25am from Plymouth to Launceston on 23 June 1962, and the signalman by the combined GWR/LSWR box is carrying the single line staff. Brent Tor is prominent in the background.

Stealing down through the woods between Cann viaduct and Plym
Bridge Platform, comes 0-6-0PT No 4658 with the Saturday 10.15am
Tavistock South to Tavistock Junction Up Yard on 17 March 1962.

On 22 December 1962 2-6-2T No 5569 is leaving Marsh Mills station to re-join the main line, for the run into Plymouth with the 12.40pm from Launceston. The notice on the right was needed because there was no footbridge.

Following closure to passengers the remaining goods line was diverted to the left, direct into Tavistock Junction Up Yard.

The last day of passenger services on the Launceston branch coincided with the start of the 'Great Freeze', and overnight snow is evident at Plymouth station on the morning of 29 December 1962, as prominent members of the Plymouth Railway Circle attach a suitable headboard to 2-6-2T No 5564 at the head of the Saturday 10.40am to Launceston. Later that day two trains were snowed-up, one at Bickleigh and the other at Tavistock South, and the last two scheduled services never even started.

Until 1945 the two 4ft 6in gauge Lee Moor Tramway Peckett 0-4-0STs had operated over the section between the inclines at Cann Wood and Torycombe. They were then locked in their shed at Torycombe until 1964, when a group of Plymouth enthusiasts took pity on them and embarked on a cosmetic restoration project on *Lee Moor No 2*, seen here outside the Torycombe shed in September 1967. This engine was later moved to Saltram House and now resides at Buckfastleigh, on the South Devon Railway.

Left: Although latterly transferred to the Western Region, the old London & South Western Railway Friary locomotive depot at Plymouth remained open until May 1963.

On 30 September 1961 ex-LSWR 'M7' class 0-4-4T No 30034 stands outside the shed, against the slate-grey rooftops of Plymouth, before working the 'last day' train to Turnchapel.

Above: An hour or so later, No 30034 is seen leaving Oreston, the first station beyond the junction with the Yealmpton branch at Plymstock, with the Plymouth Railway Circle's brake van special to Turnchapel. I must apologise for leaving my faithful 200cc LE Velocette accidentally in view.

Later on 30 September 1961, 'M7' class 0-4-4T No 30034 is leaving the river Plym bridge, on the way back to Plymouth Friary station from Turnchapel via Plymstock. The line with the level crossing gates is the ex-LSWR Cattewater branch, and bottom left is a glimpse of the Plymouth & Dartmoor Railway track near its Cattewater terminus. Cattewater Junction signalbox is in the middle distance.

The Sutton Harbour branch was visited by a Plymouth Railway Circle brake van special on 3 June 1961, hauled by 0-6-0ST No 1363. Finally closed in December 1973 and now partly used as the road access to Plymouth city centre from the Embankment, this branch was originally laid by the Plymouth & Dartmoor Railway to 4ft 6in gauge, to which was later added to the South Devon Railway's 7ft 0¼in track.

Left: Perhaps a foretaste of things to come, albeit with different motive power, if the line from Bere Alston to Tavistock is ever relaid? As 'West Country' class Pacific No 34011 *Tavistock* disappears in the distance, under a cloud of steam, with the 12.23pm from Plymouth to Tavistock, Ivatt Class 2, 2-6-2T No 41317 retrieves the rear two coaches, which are booked through to Callington, and brings them back into Bere Alston station on 1 April 1961.

Above: After travelling behind No 41317 from Bere Alston as far as the recently repainted Gunnislake station, I alighted there and was in time to see ex-LSWR class 'O2' 0-4-4T No 30225 leaving for Calstock and Bere Alston with the 1.0pm from Callington.

Left: The high northern tors of Dartmoor dominate the landscape, as BR Standard Class 4 2-6-4T No 80059 approaches across Maddaford Moor with the 3.32pm from Okehampton to Wadebridge on 4 August 1964.

Above: On 30 June 1962 Ivatt Class 2 2-6-2T No 41297 is leaving Torrington with the mid-day goods, along the line built by the North Devon & Cornwall Junction Light Railway towards Petrockstow and Meeth.

Left: At the Halwill Junction end of the ND&CJLR on 22 August 1964, Ivatt Class 2 2-6-2T No 41283 is arriving with the 8.52am from Torrington. Behind it are the 9.30am Bude to Waterloo coaches, which have been drawn out of the platform by BR Standard Class 4 2-6-4T No 80039, to await the arrival of ex-SR 'N' class 2-6-0 No 31846 with the 8.30am from Padstow, to which these coaches will then be attached.

Above: By the autumn of 1964 the motive power at Halwill Junction was changing again, with a diesel unit now on the 8.55am from Torrington, and BR Standard Class 4 4-6-0 No 75022 on the 8.48am from Padstow. BR Standard Class 4 2-6-4T No 80037 is working the 10.0am from Okehampton.

Above: At the far end of the 'Withered Arm' an ex-SR 'N' class 2-6-0 looks on from the platform at Padstow, as ex-LSWR Class T9 4-4-0 No 30709 is turned in preparation for working the 3.13pm service back to Exeter Central on 22 May 1961.

Right: On 13 July 1961 the guard of the Wenford Bridge goods stands by to close the gate at Dunmere Junction, as soon as 2-4-0 Beattie well tank No 30585 has entered the private world of the Wenford Bridge branch.

Left: Twisting with the river Camel, ex-LSWR 'O2' class 0-4-4T No 30200 hastens the 4.5pm from Bodmin North to Padstow, through the hamlet of Polbrock, near Grogley Halt, on 10 September 1960.

Above: Churchward 2-6-2T No 4565 pulls out of the delightful terminus at Bodmin General, with a single non-corridor coach forming the 12.45pm 'short working' down to Bodmin Road on the main line. This was Whit Monday 22 May 1961, an ideal time to see the banks of rhododendrons at their best.

Earlier on the afternoon of 27 May 1961, 2-6-2T No 4552 had worked two clay trains up from Boscarne Junction to Bodmin General, combined them there, and then taken the 16 loaded clays over the summit and down hill to Bodmin Road. Now, in late afternoon, it is returning to Bodmin with two sheeted wagons and a brake van. The rhododendrons are a feature of the east Cornwall railway banks.

With Moorswater viaduct striding across the valley in the background,
2-6-2T No 4552 pulls out of Coombe Junction Halt with the 5.52pm
from Liskeard to Looe on 23 May 1961.

Cornwall in Springtime — cattle and sheep graze contentedly in the fields around, as a train rolls down the valley. 2-6-2T No 4569 is between Causeland and Sandplace Halts, with the 4.35pm from Liskeard to Looe on 19 April 1960.

In the distance is Caradon Hill, the source of all the wealth, in the form of mineral ores, that created the Liskeard & Looe Union Canal, the subsequent railway and the Liskeard & Caradon Railway.

I made several visits to Looe before walking around the back of the station car park, and had meanwhile noticed that journeys back up the valley were often more sprightly than the down working.

Now it became apparent why. The engines were topping up with 'Guinness' while at Looe! 2-6-2T No 4574 is on the 10.45am to Liskeard on 2 September 1961.

Fowey No 8 Jetty as viewed from auto trailer No W193W on the 1.45pm from Fowey, while being propelled by 0-4-2T No 1468, along with trailer No W163W, back to Lostwithiel on 18 March 1961. Nowadays the rails only extend to the end of the far line of wagons, beyond which the jetties are served only by road transport, using a private road established on the trackbed of the original Cornwall Minerals Railway line from St Blazey (Par) to Fowey, including passage through Pinnock tunnel, the longest in Cornwall. Note the wagon weighbridge in the foreground.

The GWR's Lansalson branch also known as the Trenance Valley Line, which left the main line just west of St Austell, was the last to be constructed in the clay district, not being completed until 1920.

On 28 April 1962 it was visited by the Plymouth Railway Circle's 'Cornwall Minerals' brake van special hauled by 2-6-2Ts Nos 4564 and 5531.

The train is on the lower part of the line, below Bojea yard, where the engines ran around and then propelled the rest of the way. The 'whitewall' tyres on the leading vans had been acquired earlier in the day, when they paddled in liquid clay at Carbis Wharf, near Bugle.

Left: The 'Cornwall Minerals' special at St Dennis Junction, earlier in the day, after returning from Meledor Mill, at the end of the Retew branch. The engines are running around the train, prior to taking it over the also now lifted section to Parkandillack, and thence to Drinnick Mill and on down to join the main line at Burngullow. The two lines on the left are the St Dennis Junction to Tregoss Moor crossing loop on the Newquay branch.

Above: Some sections of the Newquay branch that have their roots in the original Treffry tramway are surprisingly tortuous. At milepost 299, between Quintrel Downs and St Columb Road, 4-6-0s No 7816 *Frilsham Manor* and No 6913 *Levens Hall* are negotiating a severe 'S' bend with the 12.30pm Saturdays only Newquay to Paddington service on 9 July 1960.

73

Above: There are no passengers at Mount Hawke Halt for the 4.35pm from Newquay to Chacewater, being hauled by 2-6-2T No 5562 on Monday 10 July 1961. Most of the services on this line ran through to Truro, but several relied on good connections at Chacewater into main line trains to get passengers into the city.

Right: After travelling down from Newton Abbot to Chacewater by train via Newquay (three day returns totalling 18 shillings and 2 pence)

specifically to take this view, I remember being intensely disappointed that Truro had turned out the rather careworn 2-6-2T No 5559 to haul the immaculate chocolate and cream coaches off the 8.25am from Paddington, down to Perranporth on 29 August 1959. This Saturday was the train's final run for 1959. No 5559 had been transferred from Bristol Bath Road about a year earlier and was withdrawn early in 1960.

Left: When compared with the St Ives branch, the Helston line was roughly twice as long but with only half the service. In this §fireman's eye view of Truthall Halt, two passengers are surveying the melting snow outside the 'pagoda' style shelter, as 2-6-2T No 5537 runs in with the 2.10pm from Gwinear Road to Helston on 3 March 1962.

Typical of West Cornwall are the short lengths of Barlow rail supporting the platform, a product of the West Cornwall Railway's experiment with this new and unsuccessful concept.

Above: 2-6-2T No 5537 has now arrived at Helston with the 2.10pm from Gwinear Road and 2-6-2T No 4570 is backing on from the shed road eventually to form the 3.30pm departure back to the main line.

Above: With high summer coming to a close, low tide has revealed the expanse of Porthminster beach, as 2-6-2T No 4566 leaves St Ives station behind with the 10.55am to St Erth on 9 September 1961. Three hours earlier, sister engine No 4564 had been the last engine to be prepared in St Ives shed, which closed that day. Through No 4566's exhaust can be seen the two chocolate and cream Camping Coaches and the vast length of the St Ives platform.

Right: Above the enticingly clear waters of Carbis Bay, high on the cliffs leading around to St Ives, 2-6-2T No 4570 brings a booked run-if-required set of empty stock towards St Erth, probably to provide connection with an out-of-course main line train on Saturday 19 August 1961.

Index of Locations

Ashburton branch 38, 40
Bodmin area 63, 65, 66
Brimscombe 5
Bristol (Temple Meads) 6
Callington branch 56, 57
Chacewater 75
Crowcombe (near) 14
Evercreech Junction 11
Exmouth 28
Fowey branch 70
Frome 7
Gloucester .4
Grogley Halt (near) 64
Halwill Junction 60, 61
Heathfield 29, 31
Helston branch 76, 77

Ilfracombe 18, 19
Kingsbridge branch 42, 43, 44, 45
Kingswear branch . . . . .Front cover,
. . . . .3, 32, 33, 34, 35, 36, 37
Lansalson branch 71
Launceston branch 46, 47, 48, 49
Looe branch 67, 68, 69
Lyme Regis branch 26
Maddaford Moor 58
Morebath Junction 1, 20, 21
Mount Hawke Halt 74
Newquay branch (from Par) 72, 73
Padstow 62
Plymouth Friary 52
Plymouth North Road 50
Pullabrook Halt 30

Pylle Halt 10
St Ives branch 78, 79
Sandford & Banwell 9
Sidmouth Junction 27
Sutton Harbour branch 55
Taunton 15
Thorverton 24, 25
Tiverton (near) . . . . .Back cover
Tiverton Junction 22, 23
Torrington .59
Torycombe (Lee Moor) 51
Totnes .39, 41
Turnchapel branch 53, 54
Wiveliscombe (near) 16, 17
Yatton 8
Yeovil 12, 13

PUBLISHING

Full details of Ian Allan Publishing
titles can be found on
www.ianallanpublishing.com
or by writing for a free copy of
our latest catalogue to:
Marketing Dept., Ian Allan Publishing,
Riverdene Business Park,
Molesey Road, Hersham KT12 4RG.

For an unrivalled range of aviation, military,
transport and maritime publications, visit our secure
on-line bookshop at
www.ianallansuperstore.com

or visit the Ian Allan Bookshops in
Birmingham
47 Stephenson Street, B2 4DH;
Tel: 0121 643 2496;
e-mail: ia-birmingham@btconnect.com
Cardiff
31 Royal Arcade, CF10 1AE;
Tel: 02920 390615;
e-mail: ianallancar@btconnect.com
London
45/46 Lower Marsh, Waterloo, SE1 7RG;
Tel: 020 7401 2100;
e-mail: ia-waterloo@btconnect.com
Manchester
5 Piccadilly Station Approach, M1 2GH;
Tel: 0161 237 9840;
e-mail: ia-manchester@btconnect.com

and (aviation and military titles only) at the **Aviation
Experience,
Birmingham International Airport**
3rd Floor, Main Terminal, B26 3QJ;
Tel: 0121 781 0921
e-mail: ia-bia@btconnect.com

or through mail order by writing to:
Ian Allan Mail Order Dept.,
4 Watling Drive, Hinckley LE10 3EY.
Tel: 01455 254450.
Fax: 01455 233737.
e-mail: midlandbooks@compuserve.com

You are only a visit away from over 1,000
publishers worldwide.